When Gnats Swarm

When Gnats Swarm

They Swarmed Like Groups of Graft on the Innocent

RoseMary Martin

authorHOUSE®

AuthorHouse™
1663 Liberty Drive
Bloomington, IN 47403
www.authorhouse.com
Phone: 1 (800) 839-8640

Published by AuthorHouse 09/28/2019

ISBN: 978-1-4634-0233-4 (sc)

Library of Congress Control Number: 2011908263

FIRST EDITION

Front Cover Design by RoseMary Martin.
Photography by: Common Wikimedia, Dragonfly Green—Eyed Hawker.

Contents

Authors Note and Biography

The author writes the book "When Gnats Swarm" which sets a true adventure of her early grandfather's life as the events took place when a trip to Germany to visit family became tragic. In the book which the author writes, has three true stories written from author of a little girls view and the story leads to how the mis-fortunate came at a young age within a family. The author writes of the Hitler era when her grandfather, grandmother, mother and uncle left Virginia to visit the old relatives with passport in hand and to return, when suddenly the war broke out in Germany. A family stuck in the paths of destiny from the day forward. This for the first time is brought to you with the author's knowledge and private collection left to her and years gathered to bring to you the book "When Gnats Swarm" and what one man could not tell.

The author grew up in a rural way as life seemed different as others came through depressions or didn't in time. Curiously, noticing between two countries, the history of depression was different, the author noticed, with the effects war on society. Her interests grew about society and their depressions of war. The author writes the followings through time, into three stories.

WELCOME TO

WHEN GNATS SWARM

Preface

A JOURNEY YOU'LL NEVER FORGET. A story of the innocent surrounded with cruel and injustice behavior of the plots of fraud. IvoryRose is pulled in an assemblage of what many have seeked to conquer. A man who sought for injustice, falls into the foes of fraud and becomes entangled with the swarm of the incompetence game of fraud. As the biggest bust unfolds in lag of a Universe, is now her story written. The day Hanson will never forget is about to unfold in his life. A swarm of fraud so big no world could see beyond the destruction to dismantle. A fraud lead for centuries, became a *swarm of gnats* and spread across to worlds of peace. A fraud that hindered the young and old, the good and bad could not untangle the movement of ones fate. A trap of all time waits, like a hunter's hole in the ground. IvoryRose found the culprits who you have once gloomed into their swarm and lost. You fell in heart and never saw their lies in front. They tormented with you, took your money and ran like a thief. Their true behavior edged each note written for more. You await, for the fraud have swarmed in groups of graft on the innocent in *The Gnats Swarm.*

Distant Peace

IvoryRose, a delighted woman of respect, who would seek her dreams of wonder. A swarm of dragonflies would enter her head filled with swarms of a whimsical buzz. A distance of an unknown place would pull her near but not far as she stood knowing her distant peace of nature. So amazing the sound of the natures swarm and the magnetic thought calling in the distant sky across, which she never forgot.

Beginning the rival of a new day, the dreams of a swarm stayed. IvoryRose made her usual entrance into the day opening the french-doors and walking onto the deck of what was a house nestled in the mountain trees. What seemed a tree house, became curious indeed of what was to come. IvoryRose told of her Cherokee decent of her fore great grandfather's marriage to a Cherokee woman of the Wicomico area of Indians yearned to be in the Mountains of her true ancestors. Living near her fiancée, she learned no day was without the outside world she saw in his field of law.

It was 3 am when a call came, as Hanson reached his phone to the side of his bed. Hello this is Hanson. The dark room was quiet and reserved of the night call.

Again he asked, Barrister Charmer Kokee hello, with a hesitant sound quickly, not let the caller hang up. How are you tonight, sir? I will do that right now. Hello, hello. He hung up on me, Hanson exclaimed. It's 3:08am and he hung up the phone. At the very moment the phone rang again. Hanson picked up the phone. Hello. Barrister Charmer Kokee, just a moment I will get a paper and pen. A number was written as I looked, what seemed a foreign country code. Ok sir, I will do that now and Hanson hung the phone up. IvoryRose asked who was Barrister Charmer Kokee and why was he calling at 3 am in fear? This is the man who was calling for weeks I told you about waking me up every night at 3 and 4am with information from Terri, he exclaimed. This a first experience, IvoryRose knew there was more to the call. As never to question Hanson's client business, IvoryRose felt, this would in time. Hanson walked to his computer. I asked what are you seeking Hanson? Hanson exclaimed, an email from the Barrister Charmer Kokee, and he left the room. Moments later Hanson returned with a piece of paper. Please read this IvoryRose. As she sat up Hanson left the room to pour a glass of wine. The note was a receipt that Hanson was to handle an endowment or account of $6.7million dollars to help a woman who could not have inherited her father's estate according to the Gigeria laws. The woman was portrayed by Hanson as a classmate of law during his studies in college. The woman Tracy Livingston who traveled across with her family to Gigeria was said to have a tragic loss of her parents, in a dinning restaurant in Gigeria, was seeking Hanson's law help. As most of Tracy's claim to Hanson seemed bazaar, IvoryRose asked Hanson what happened to Tracy's parents and husband? One evening Tracy, her husband and parents were dinning at a restaurant table in Gigeria when an unknown amount of men busted in the doors and began shooting at the table where Tracy was seated, said Hanson. Three at the table died and one survived. The survivor was Tracy as Hanson claimed. After weeks of hospital stay, Tracy remembering Hanson was an attorney in the USUS, searched for Hanson's phone number and called, Hanson exclaimed. The call entailed, her father's estate of 6.7 million dollars of which Tracy's bank of Rinky in that country was not allowing her father's funds to be inherited to a woman. Tracy found Hanson and wanted him to inherite the estate as Tracy felt give it to Hanson and not Gigeria a dime of her father's monies. Then considering the situation Hanson learned, and who sounded like Tracy from his past, Hanson took on the account of the Rinky Bank as his lawful job and begin writing to Rinky Bank government officials of OCE. The endowment to transfer rightfully, would be started into Hanson's new account of which he began a company, for the children in need of health care. As this agreement was Tracy's wish and stipulation, for the endowment to Hanson.

The Hospital

The recovery took sometime before Tracy could call out to Hanson for updates on the release of the estate. Form after form was requested from OCE government officials and Rinky bank. One day in Hanson's study, an email came from Tracy. It stated in her email, "not to write to her for now" because the hospital missionary had her computer and missionaries showing up at her room. Tracy told Hanson to get her out of the hospital as she was in danger. Hanson called the Barrister Charmer Kokee who was in Gigeria to fly Tracy out immediately to a safer place. The Barrister Charmer Kokee who claimed he lived in London, booked a flight that evening for two. Tracy was extremely sick and could hardly get out of bed, but prepared to leave to London in hours. And they left to London. Tracy was sure the missionary man was the group who shot her parents and husband as she claimed to Hanson on the phone. Now the calls to Hanson were coming from London. One evening around 1am a call from Tracy came. IvoryRose could hear the voice, so loud and was crying because she may not get the release from the bank of the 6.7 million. Hanson aher he will get the release and place the monies to the non-profit children fund. This seemed all Tracy wanted. Emails were coming in the study computer stating it was Tracy, but Tracy was in London with Barrister Charmer Kokee by country code calls. The emails were sentimental sexual gestures asking Hanson did he miss her and how much she needed Hanson in her life and signed, Tracy. As the situation was turning more bazaar, Hanson decided to go get the endowment himself and continue the bureaucratic efforts, but not tell Barrister Charmer Kokee as if it was a game each were playing. Certificate after certificate came and copy after copy was kept, still no release of 6.7 million to help children of cancer. So a date was set to meet the officials of the endowment. Hanson became sick and tried to finalize the transfer. Arguments began between Hanson and Tracy.

In A Whimsical Moment

The process became slower. A statement came from Rinky Bank exclaiming the release was coming but not through wire transfer as set. The monies would arrive from Zinatia to Quebece in one week with no more transfer costs; then to have Quebece transfer. Hanson was thrilled and claimed "this is it" but I'm too sick to go IvoryRose. Now it is time to deposit and meet who the Barrister Charmer Kokee was dealing with, the Zanatia in Quebece. Surely all was official, claimed IvoryRose to Hanson? Yes, claimed Hanson, everything is set. The flight and hotel will be paid. Would you go just to sign the transfer to the bank who I already set up the account for me? IvoryRose knew Hanson worked very hard to the estate transfer and offered to settle the account along with a power of attorney in hand, the Port-a-Security for safety and so the conference room and hotel was scheduled in a Quebece hotel. All was prepared and ready. One week later, IvoryRose went to collect and deposit 6.7 million dollars arriving in Quebece. The next morning at 9:00 am a woman was to arrive at the conference room and IvoryRose was to count 6.7 million dollars. Instead a call came. It was Hanson. Hello

IvoryRose, I just got a call from Miss Wicker and she cannot meet you. IvoryRose exclaimed no changes in the plan Hanson, it makes me nervous with so much monies pending with your endowment! Mr. Smith is on his way and should be there in 20 minutes. I don't like it Hanson, she exclaimed. There it was, very little time to back out and come so far to settle the endowment in minutes Port-a-Security at her door, IvoryRose waited 40 minutes and a little slim beady-eyed man in a suit appeared. I'm Mr. Smith. Do you have your power of attorney? Yes, Mr. Smith and showed him the power of attorney as he did not spend a second looking. Ok, Mr. Smith do you have an ID, said IvoryRose? I will show you my ID when we are finished counting the 6.7 million and you sign the paper release. The red flags went up as high as can be. IvoryRose wanted justice to prevail for the beady eyed man, running the exchange time of transfer, IvoryRose had never counted so many monies, but planned each stack amount she would count while on the plane, to make the count quickly. Mr. Smith asked what are the guards about? They are my personal guards, exclaimed IvoryRose. Mr. Smith exclaimed abruptly, ask them to leave. IvoryRose knew this man was not a banker. IvoryRose assured him the guards were only to protect her and were no harm to him. Mr. Smith then changed the room to counting the estate monies in a room upstairs and no guard around. The estate had already been in Hanson's name. IvoryRose afraid the man would walk out and such a long trip to meet them and many efforts to transfer the money was becoming less and less a chance, so IvoryRose agreed no guard. Just before Mr. Smith left, he told IvoryRose a man from Zanatia would bring the monies in and Mr. Smith would have a paper to sign after counting and wait downstairs. The only plan told to IvoryRose was for Mr. Smith to greet and make sure the connection was met and the release of the document would be signed. Minutes later, IvoryRose in the room heard a knock at the door and hands sweating, opened the door.

It was the guard. Her heart relieved he was still there. The guard told IvoryRose to inspect the bill in the middle of the stacks and he left. Another knock, IvoryRose wanted to fly back the very minute. This time Zanatia was at the door. A stocky man entered sweating and humped over pulling a dark suitcase on wheels about two feet wide by two and a half feet deep. Put the bag in the corner and stand in the back of the room please, exclaimed IvoryRose. Zanatia man stood up and started coming forward. Are you afraid of me or afraid I would stab you? No I just think you might stab me, exclaimed IvoryRose. The man then bent over to unzip the bag, one side and then the other. There it was 6.7 million, she knew by the size of the stacks already figured on the plane. Each stack of USUS 100 dollar bills wrapped in clear wrap neatly one stack on top of each in four rows and several deep. The man bending over guarding and hovering the wad, was not allowing IvoryRose close. IvoryRose asked may I see one bill? Ok, as the man reached at the top pack pointing. See? No I don't see, I want the middle stack. As the man reached for the second row, IvoryRose exclaimed I want to pick the bill. Ok, he exclaimed. As she reached to the top layer she watched the man yet ready to call the guard, she found four layer down stack, grabbed then, pulled. The man took the pack and opened the clear plastic. The man reached for the top bill. Again IvoryRose shook her head with prepared to call guards fearing his turn, and the man suddenly reached in and pulled a $100 dollar bill, gave it to IvoryRose.

IvoryRose inspected the bill but it did not seem good yet, she was not sure. Quietly, she stood ready to count the bills as planned, she began to sweat and the man started gathering the stack, putting it back quickly. While zipping the sides, IvoryRose still holding the 100 dollar bill, the man suddenly started walking out the room. The man was very nervous and IvoryRose called to him. "Where is the paper for me to sign?" The man hustling down the hotel hall pulling the 6.7 million suitcase behind him turns and says, I'll be right back. The guard still standing at the door as the man left sweeping by, the guard asked IvoryRose, what she wanted them to do. IvoryRose knowing this man will not return said drive me to the closest bank and to verify the $100.00 bill. The second guard at the front hotel door must have seen the car leave. IvoryRose hoped the guard out front would follow the two men as Mr. Smith had already disappeared and IvoryRose did not know where he went and the two men could not be found. IvoryRose immediately called Hanson and told him what happened with the Zanatia man who showed the endowment Hanson was working on. It was real IvoryRose exclaimed! It was dawning on her it would have to be a bust at that point and wanted Hanson to call security to send after the culprits. IvoryRose tried to convey to Hanson the monies so real, before her. The guard only saw a $100.00 bill, a stocky man leaving with a suitcase and knowledge of the endowment claimed by Hanson, an attorney.

The decisions came as quickly as IvoryRose felt, was this a setup Hanson did not understand after $ 20,800.00 to get the transfer established and initiated? The legalities were set according to Hanson. Was he legal she began to think and were these Zanatia men more but fraud? The guards and IvoryRose set off toward the bank not knowing if the fraud men would follow. Not knowing who else was around the hotel how much more corruption was about to take place. What did Mr. Smith and the girl missing at the meeting from NY. have to do with the Hansons endowment?

The Arrival—The Bank

Approaching the manager walking through the large entrance with the guard beside IvoryRose, she explained the power of attorney, the amount possible to deposit, Hanson's previous calls to the bank, the account already open for Hanson's deposit for the children and the $100.00 to verify. The bank took the $100.00 USUS monies and in 15 minutes approached IvoryRose. And with what she waited for was imperative to Hanson's endowment. It is fine IvoryRose the manager exclaimed. IvoryRose looked up into the room and sighed for she knew Hanson could not have transitioned the transfer himself, but the money was real. Port-a-Security escorted IvoryRose to another location and guarded the door all night. By morning security would escort IvoryRose back to the airport for return home. The 100 dollar-bill was still in the possession of IvoryRose. Finally meeting Hanson, she showed the 100 dollar bill copied at the bank. By the ordeal, Port-A-Security had noted with the day unfolding, indeed an endowment for a company already set for the children legally was unfolding. Still a scheme now seemed prominent to the connection of the culprits, as IvoryRose was now concluding. Hanson had to decide what now must he do she thought? Was he to walk away or still believe a fraud? Barrister Charmer Kokee never mentioned or knew yet of the endowment transaction which took place in Quebece. Was Barrister Charmer Kokee baffled? Hanson began to tell Barrister Charmer Kokee of the transaction and for Barrister Charmer Kokee to do his job and transfer the monies into Hanson's USUS account by the day. Again the Rinky Bank of Gigeria, Barrister Charmer Kokee and OCE showing a process of certificates of mailings to Hanson changed, from the first request from Hanson to wire into his USUS account to instead a foreign visa card. A prior bank code did not work from the two banks with thousands of dollars Hanson sank into the transfer. The USUS bank of choice gave the wrong number code to Hanson so a red flag went up in the foreign Rinky Bank. The code was written on back of a bank business card but was incorrectly written which later Hanson questioned and held the bank accountable after Hanson wrote a letter to the top official of the USUS bank who thought it was fraud, of his findings which related to the now loss of endowment and Hanson's own personnel bank account held for years. With the wrong code written from the USUS bank caused confusion. Was it fraud? Now the foreign bank suddenly required a Visa card be sent to Hanson holding the endowment at the Rinky Bank against Hanson's wishes to use a visa card with a code. The card was issued to Hanson via mail against his wishes of which a code Hanson kept. The card apparently fits only a Rinky Bank in Gigneria. The thick card now established in Hanson's name was released to him and can only be released through a Gigneria Bank of which the card can only work. The Barrister Charmer

Kokee had a card set only for Gigneria, but concludes Visa Debit on the card and the card should work also in the USUS as an International Visa but did not according to legalities. The endowment sits again in Hanson's name. Hanson tried to get the Barrister Charmer Kokee to transfer the funds without any more cost to his USUS account. The USUS bank did not accept the thick card and claimed the account must still be at the foreign bank or Visa account company in Hanson's account. Hanson's health became worse and frustration and began to take a toll on Hanson's business to finalize the promise to a friend? After two tries and a try with Hanson's USUS bank, the thick card, did not work. The Barrister Charmer Kokee still calling Hanson became less between the two however; the Barrister Charmer Kokee was trying to hang on a communication with Hanson when the transfer became locked into the foreign debit card in Hanson's account. The account may be set to draw interest for Hanson's account. Would they claim Hanson's interest too? The claim for the USUS citizen's endowment for a USUS non-profit company legally noted and account established, was a legal request to transfer of 6.7 million. The visa card which never worked in a USUS bank, could not process a withdrawal transfer from the card to Hanson's USUS account as a business holder. The illegal Rinky Bank is holding a business fraud bank and does not release to the legal card holder its funds, intentionally. When the calls were confirmed to the Rinky Bank, why didn't the banker investigate the account of wrong doing with so many calls? The illegal Rinky Bank can never own Hanson's account which is in his name and sits across the seas. The phone numbers were answered by the representative as the business title of the bank. Again, wanting more process and monies. As the issued card can only be used in the foreign country, who issued and documented to the account. IvoryRose knew Hanson's request could only be for the endowment but why did he not lead on about their fraud or certainly seemed to bust a fraud. Could this be a fraud endowment or an actual endowment? The bank number stopped working.

In the days leading up to a universal bust of fraudulent encounters and with the Barrister Charmer Kokee still delaying Hanson's transaction to this day, IvoryRose decided to encourage Hanson to write to the Skotlake Grounds in hopes to catch the culprits. As the Barrister Charmer Kokee favored a set-up earlier for Hanson which never took place, it would not be hard to find them by the Zant group found in Quebece, who bit the ring. Hanson sat a moment as he starred at the address to Scotlake Ground, IvoryRose began to wonder if he knew what she had been through at the front line of a culprit swarm days ago. How much danger was lurking in the moment of their swarms standing before the arm of the beast. The front man showed up suddenly, by emailing Hanson trying to control the transaction, the moment with an international number from Gigeria calling. A person came on the same line claiming to be from Officials of the Rinky Bank. The associate Mr. Greenery a so called official of the Rinky Bank, was jerking and baiting the transaction between Barrister Charmer Kokee and Hanson trying to control by intervening the endowment by adding thousands for transporting the 6.7 million, days before the trip. Then an agreement was set between Barrister Charmer Kokee and Hanson with Barrister Charmer Kokee and Mr. Greenery the monies would be limited to less in the first transfer to Hanson. Even so,

IvoryRose at first front saw what looked like 6.7 million in the black wheeled suitcase as half did not arrive.

As Hanson began to type, the anger building in IvoryRose as she had realized the crooked thieves Hanson was dealing in, made her sick to her stomach and was not one to be backed to a wall. Watching him type the story directly to be sent immediately via email to Scotlake, IvoryRose knew Hanson did agreed reporting the culprits as she encouraged him strongly. IvoryRose with the respect she had for Hanson in his duties, was an eye opening for what was not the person she met or was he? The candle burns as so does the flame but the flame was hot. The flame turns as a tornado whips the wind. IvoryRose was in an uncomfortable zone, as those moments seemed something perhaps in a movie than, to face such culprits before knowing their intentions. Was she too falling in their swarm? Not on your life as she knew their fraud but became tangled in Hansons blind love. How long do you know a man, IvoryRose thought of the months gone by and began to quickly summon up the real man before her. Was he a man to help for a rightful deed? Nevertheless; the story was written as Hanson turned with a nervous look in his eyes and said, "this man will hunt". And hunt he did when another email came in from the Barrister Charmer Kokee asking for more deposit for the transfer. Hanson refused. Do your job Barrister Charmer Kokee, he exclaimed as he did many times. Transfer the funds! The endowment in Hanson's name was immediate according to the official documents on file. All requests through the banks, the legal attorney documents, letters, signatures and company children account have been filed and accepted legally through both countries including the Barrister Charmer Kokee in London. How much more of this Hanson, IvoryRose told Hanson? Please don't send another dime, exclaimed IvoryRose. Hanson agreed and no more monies was sent to the culprits. Hanson would smile like a relief of justice suddenly encountered. IvoryRose thought how much more could thieves take in their swarm? So forth was the obstruction to the innocent, where was the authorities and security who stood before her? Was security finding them or were they onto them?

The Montreel trip was not forgotten. IvoryRose knows how to bait the culprits and hoping security would allow her the next move. IvoryRose grew an anger by these culprits and she wanted justice to prevail. The letter to Scotlake Grounds would be the start. Would they ever contact her or Hanson? IvoryRose knew she could bait the culprits to this day, as she knows what the culprits bite too. It was the largest anarchic of catch, the moment before security, IvoryRose and the law faced the culprits. Face to face, head on as she watched the moment unfold.

A Moment in control

The OEC officers or claimed officers in Gigeria coordinated many approvals for the Rinky Bank associated with now Hanson's endowment. The calls started to double day and night between Hanson and Barrister Charmer Kokee. Now that Hanson's endowment sits in a Gigerian Visa in Hanson's name was intentionally locked to the Visa account without Hanson's consent. Nevertheless; the endowment is Hanson's legally and rightfully. Would the real card fit the international country bank (s)? The evening turned as the call with Barrister Charmer Kokee usually calm, was again requesting more deposit to transfer the card to Hanson's USUS company established account. Hanson claimed, his patience was running thin. What was Hanson about to do, thought IvoryRose? Was all hell about to break other than in Quebece; when IvoryRose was confronted with the dangerous culprits? There was the danger, a man standing in a small room alone before her with 6.7 million and what if a gun was hidden? It was more than time the culprits were stopped! IvoryRose left on travel when a call came to Hanson from an investigator in Scotlake. Invy spoke with Hanson of the incidents which occurred in his transactions. Names, places and individuals were noted. Two weeks later, Hanson called IvoryRose and again claimed, this dog will hunt", yes hunt he did. The Barrister Charmer Kokee was in jail in London held for questioning, he claimed, from the investigator who spoke to Hanson by phone. The biggest universal bust ever was unfolding as the Barrister Charmer Kokee claiming to uphold law was in jail, claimed Hanson. Where was the girl now who hung the phone up when IvoryRose called asking for Barrister Charmer Kokee. The number to London still worked. Was the girl Terry, Terry? Was she alright? IvoryRose traveling to Hanson's home bypassing bears stopped in the driveway and parked. Hanson came to the door as he always did expecting IvoryRose and waited as she entered the large room to give her news of the Barrister Charmer Kokee. IvoryRose took her suitcase downstairs and settled by the fireplace and offered a glass of wine. The evening was different as Hanson became quiet and sick. The day wore on him as he had wine and stayed in his study. Later IvoryRose went to bed to wake up and the light was still on in the study. Hanson was on the phone. IvoryRose could hear a conversation between a girl and Hanson as she walked to the study. A conversation between a girl and Hanson went on a short time. The phone hung up. IvoryRose asked who it was? A girl I represented in Texas, exclaimed Hanson. Really, at 3am in the morning Hanson. Off to bed he went staggering and falling on the corner bed leaving gouges and blood he never felt, as he exclaimed. I was in a nightmare to untangle, thought IvoryRose. She walked back to the study as Hanson slept and found a paper printed on his desk. It was emails from the girl in Texas and emails from Terry in London. The London email was addressed as "Honey, I miss you". When are you coming?

IvoryRose nearly dropped her jaw. Sensual gestures went back and forth. The next day IvoryRose asked Hanson of the email from London? It is Terry's sister. The letter had a picture of Terry with very little clothing on. That morning as IvoryRose settled in by the fireplace a call came. It was not answered but a message was left and herd across the room. Hi baby, this is Gi Gi, I'm in room 2. Call me. Love you. Huh, IvoryRose exclaimed! Who was that Hanson? A girl I use to date once, met her at a vitamin convention. Anymore, Hanson, she asked? Did you meet many? I got a call once from a very wealthy woman who flew me out to represent her in her divorce, Hanson exclaimed. I was her attorney for a short time. IvoryRose became quiet. That evening as IvoryRose settled downstairs another call came and Hanson upstairs picked the phone up. Hi baby! I will come sometime to Texas, as he exclaimed. IvoryRose having no reason for doubt who these people were calling and late at night began to doubt his trust. Who was the girl emailing? The calls were repeatedly coming so IvoryRose headed back to her home. Hanson kept emailing IvoryRose of how awful for her to leave. IvoryRose thought perhaps he is right and invited Hanson to visit and discuss the calls. One week after Hanson arrived he became very sick and left his phone sitting in the kitchen. The phone rang and IvoryRose saw the number and saw many of the same numbers left on his phone. It was certain the two were getting together. IvoryRose told Hanson to get a flight back home and seek a Doctor. Not letting on to the calls. Hanson left the next day. Still writing to IvoryRose exclaiming his Doctor visits, the Barrister Charmer Kokee calling and a new puppy he got. Days later a call came to IvoryRose from one of Hanson's neighbors. Hanson is in the hospital, I have been trying to find your number. It was Monday when the call came and Hanson was then put on life support that afternoon and died Wednesday.

~

The Hunting

As the gnats still swarm, the dog will hunt. As Hanson set the ball rolling, IvoryRose followed the next turn. Hanson's email at her home became quiet. Weeks later, an email came from London. It was from Barrister Charmer Kokee asking for Hanson to email him as it was very important. IvoryRose blocked the emails from London to all of Rinky officials. Little did they know, the hunt is still on. The stacks of official notices from attorneys, legal files and payments are noted for an endowment to be inherited legally now to Hanson's preference in his will. As the rights to an estate, all funds go to the inherited. So does the international visa can only be used by the original holder, a male inheritance? And what next, from a fraud scheme does a fraud official claim on the account? Interest? If the card works in their international bank then; will the inherited own 6.7million? More processing is not due from the fraud swarm only legal hands can purvey of his legal side. The dogs hunt! And so he did! And so did she.

The Story of IvoryRose

Preface

The gentle sound of the Virginia surf lacing the beach was soothing to IvoryRose and Hanson. They had awaited the moment through months of love, during most of which they were apart from each other's tender hugs and passionate kisses. The couple met by happenstance almost a year before. Because of jobs and geography, they had devoted time to each other, but 450 miles apart.

The cool September sand beneath their feet was comfortable and conducive to love. The seagulls had long before settled in for the evening. The night sky was ablaze with stars. The Chesapeake Bay was alight by the beacons of freighters and navel vessels coming and going. The ocean breeze on their faces had a comforting influence on the couple, very much love showed on their faces.

The IvoryRose Story

Hanson reached out to his hoped for bride, took her hands and gently asked IvoryRose to marry him and spend the rest of her life in his arms. He was very much in love. As he placed the engagement ring on her delicate finger, Hanson said, "My IvoryRose, I love you. I ask you to marry me. Let me spend the rest of our lives as your husband and you as my wife."

"Our love is enduring," IvoryRose responded. "I could never have fallen in love with a better man than you. I would be blessed to be your wife. As she placed the ring on his finger made of silver and black with a small arrow engraved, beside a center diamond. "Lets keep this for now" for time will grow our love?

"Our love is enduring," IvoryRose responded. Their love was official, and they could now begin planning the rest of their lives together.

Ivory Rose had been previously married for 17 years and Hanson for 21. Divorce had been painful for the two, but absolutely necessary, they felt, long before they met each other. The two had now come to know real, genuine love with each together.

The couple spent time in each others arms before retiring for the evening to admire the symbols of their love. Their pillow talk lasted for several hours, with both all smiles.

The two were charmed by each other and by the water. They shared a Virginia heritage. Neither wanted the exchanging of rings and pledges to take place in a crowded, fancy restaurant, as was the local custom, and in no other place than Virginia. They wanted the privacy and solitude of a beach. With sand between their toes, the beach and surf was the ideal backdrop for the most special time in their relationship. The two kissed passionately and held each other for a long time.

As the sun pushed its way across the next day morning sky, Hanson and IvoryRose awakened to the idea of having breakfast catered by room service. A double order of eggs, toast, grape jelly, orange juice and coffee was perfect for their palate.

While awaiting delivery of breakfast, the couple walked IvoryRose canine companion, Zumann, who had permission from the hotel to share the room. Zumann, a fawn-colored Pekingese, seemed to sense that something special was underway. He bounced across the sand like he was experiencing a new day. He was. And so were IvoryRose and Hanson.

The Porch

In her bathrobe in the gently swaying front porch swing, Vera watched as her daughter, IvoryRose made her way back to the house through the warm summer sand along the Potomac River in southern Maryland. The gulls were having their early morning feeding while a school of porpoises was doing the same, only several feet off the beach.

On her early morning walk, IvoryRose had collected a pocketful of periwinkles, which in Texas are purple flowers growing along the roadsides. In the Bay area, though, periwinkles are actually barnacles with mussels in them. She was thinking of how delicious her mother's coffee and pancakes would be to start the day. IvoryRose was also thinking of her desire to truly have a special love in her life.

"Look at these, mother. Aren't they gorgeous?" Rose exclaimed about her collected periwinkles. I couldn't find many clams or oyster shells, but these periwinkles were everywhere. I had such a nice walk. It's so good to be here."

They're beautiful, honey. What would you like for breakfast?"

"I was hoping for blueberry or banana pancakes. You make them so well. If you'll make the pancakes, I'll warm the syrup and get the coffee maker going. Do we have orange juice?"

"Of course, dear. You know I don't like to add fruit to the cakes, but I will for you. I love you so much, honey. You seem so very calm and relaxed. Let's make a deal. I will make the pancakes if you will prepare the coffee and heat up the maple syrup. It's from Vermont. Flown into the market just last week. You can also set the table and pour the orange juice, if you don't mind." "You know I will. I love having breakfast with you near the water."

In the kitchen, the pair set about their jobs. Vera fired up the range and Ivory clattered with the plates and tableware. The maple syrup began to heat slowly, just as the first pancake was coning out of the pan.

"How many would you like, honey?" Vera asked.

"Three will be more than enough."

"Would you like some sausage with it?

"Heavens no,' IvoryRose Said. "With the pancakes you make, along with the coffee and juice, why that will be a gracious plenty.

"Honey, I'm so glad you are back with me on the family land. You know our heritage goes back in two distinct directions. To Germany through your grandfather and also to the Cherokee. The Indians were here in southern Maryland long before the English and other settlers ever set foot in southern Maryland."

"I know, Mom, and I intend to research that further real soon. I want to know the details of my heritage and want to learn as much as I can about it".

"It's a proud and honorable heritage, my love." Vera said softly".

"What about the Amish, Mom?" IvoryRose asked.

"Well, it's like this, honey. Part of the Amish came and settled and lived on our farm. After your father died we sold the farm to the Amish. You should study up about them, they are good people. Like our family, they originated in Germany."

The Amish people seem to be devoutly spiritual, keeping to themselves and don't bother anyone. I run into them at the market. They sell their produce and milk, hitch up their wagons and go home. I cannot be Amish, but I am sometimes envious of the privacy they enjoy."

"Honey, like our family, the Amish are of German descent. Let's enjoy our pancakes. You've poured the coffee and juice, and set the table. We have plenty of time to talk."

Breakfast for Two

Sitting at the small breakfast table for two, the pair spent moments in silence, sipping their coffee and think about what had been and what could be. For now though, they were living in the present.

"You know, sweetie, yuour daddy would have been proud of you. He loved this fertile land and he adored the water, but died doing what he loved. I'm so sad that you hardly got to know him."

IvoryRose father had been a salty dog fisherman on the Chesapeake Bay and farmed. He met an untimely death in an accident while trying to untangle a fishing line in knots. He dove from the fishing vessel, worked with the lines trying to salvage his catch and was pulled down by the strong undertow.

"I honestly can't remember my dad. What was he like, Mom?"

"Oh, he had a range of personalities. He was a tall and warm man. Dieter was my prince. He was a man to truly love, honey. He was passionate about his fishing, but he would sulk about missed opportunities.

"I did not know if I could survive after his death as this area did not have much in jobs for woman". It was very far to the city and with two children to raise I settled as a waitress. I felt for a while that the emotions were going to get the best of me. But here I am today having pancakes with my darling daughter, the very best that your dad and I could have ever done."

The two sat quietly for a while, sipping their coffee. The pancakes had been polished off. IvoryRose liked just two sugars in her java and Vera liked only crème.

"Mom, do you think I will ever love again. Maybe God wants me to be alone. Maybe I will."

"Stop talking like that honey. Just be patient and, at the right time, your true soul mate will knock on the door and if you invite him, he will come into your life".

"I always feel so good sharing my feelings with you, Mom. What more can you tell me about my grandfather Opa?"

"Well, he was a wonderful goldsmith and jeweler in east Germany, his fathers were silversmiths. He made only the finest jewelry. Your Opa was a strong man, but he had a delicate and precise touch with things that are so special to fine women like us. I don't want to put us on a pedestal as anything special, but we are not like the people around the Bay now. This used to be our land and our turf.

Unfortunately, people are now coming on land that our family once owned and, whew, they are different. Be careful around them, dear."

The two sat quietly for moments, until IvoryRose broke the silence.

"I want to fall in love with a strong man that will stand tall when challenged, but yet one who is tender with my feelings. Do you feel there are still men out there like that?"

"Of course I do. Don't be deceived by fellows who come along wanting to buy your favor, showing off their fancy cars and houses. Those can go away in a New York minute. You and I both know what they want. You could be a trophy bride for some, but please don't go there. You could marry again, belong to the finest country club, go to the nicest cocktail parties and pretend you were happy."

IvoryRose sat calmly and reflected on the sage advice from her mother and thought, it would be fun to dress up. She did not want to live the rest of her life alone, but knew her mother was guiding her in the right direction. "Could I take care of the dishes, Mom?"

"Of course not, honey. This is my house and these are my dishes. I enjoyed lour breakfast and our conversations. Let's do this more often. Just go sit on the porch and think about what we discussed."

"Thank you, mom, I love you so very much."

"I love you too honey."

A little girl growing in a warm sense of a home had more than a no where land. As a young girl, learned environments were different as people grew toward what their ground is today. A broad vision produced her mind of new and different habitat in an open world. The warm of the day soon became a vision in mind. The strings surrounding her and gliding the air five feet away, gave the little girl her love to natures ground. A string would be tied around the little June bug to fly in circles but soon let loose to fly unhurt. The sound of wings humming in the air, was like a child circling to play in the fields in nature. *IvoryRose* patience was thin to play June bug again. As the next day rose, she picked up her string left by the back door and went into the warm day looking for Mr. June bug. There he was bigger than ever. As she reached in the air to catch the June bug, a distant sound was heard. The sound was so catching to mind, like a hum in the air. Not a bird but a sound of different wing flying in swarm. IvoryRose heard a calling with curiosity, within a soft humming sound of wings. As IvoryRose grew into a woman remembering her childhood plays of fun and the sound of the wings humming in mind, she heard the sounds again. Again, it was one summer day in a field when IvoryRose looked up and followed the sound of flapping wings. Almost whimsical the soft sound was a swarm of dragonflies. That was it, the same sound she heard in her childhood, wings flapping. But how does it seem so distant, still, yet so far? A huge force she felt surrounding her, like knowing herself, for the first time. Yet with all this happening it was like being close to the love ones she once knew. IvoryRose as a child experienced early grief of love ones from her father dying by drowning in the beautiful bay at the age of 1 ½ years. She did not remember a father figure but a shadow of a man in memory. One and a half years later, IvoryRose felt grief of her dearest father figure, her grandfather Opa died suddenly. The Grandfather was the closest male figure to the little girl growing up in a love family. It was through her Grandfather she learned about part of the world by what he left, a huge array of knowledge. The sound of many wings in a very distant place was unknown, to her. So curious, she began to search dragonfly's origin. The African fields, that's it! A distant place so far but a connection was pulling her like a magnet. Always fascinated by the dragonfly, IvoryRose felt something else connected. It was years before she understood a connection.

IvoryRose grew with a love with children and with people who loved children. IvoryRose was taught to think of lost children. At age 5 she went on a trip with her family to an orphanage for the first time on a pleasant day driving hours into the hills with so much color bursting in color and saw the day as fun and new.

IvoryRose Mother was the greatest inspiration and sun in her life giving her insight of love. The orphanage with children ages infant to 3 years was packed with cribs in a large room. As IvoryRose walked in at age 8, a small little girl near two reached through the medal prongs etched with scratches and looked into IvoryRose eyes with a sad appearance. The little girl in the crib had such an influence over IvoryRose, she never forgot the little girl arms reaching. IvoryRose could hardly walk away but remembered the little girl to this day with thoughts of hope to children in the world. The thoughts of this little girl and care from her Mother, IvoryRose found a passion for the suffering and young. She grew up wanting to help and a passion behind her, but the means did not come until one day later. Always reaching but nothing came. IvoryRose knew something was behind her and someday it would come. The scars of life which left memories from her Opa captured on return to the US, his home. The father figure so kind she knew. The way for him was part her now. A family owned business in Virginia and Grandfathers before became the love of her life with a little store settled in a block village with a big picture window one could feast their eyes on, glowing of crystal, silver, clocks, porcelain, gold and whimsical sounds surrounded the room as she entered. The morning day was IvoryRose walking into the store watching the glitter of light flickering across the room and her Oma standing behind the counter, she would be shinning silver teapots. The little man through the narrow door in the corner, would sit behind a bench with dye cast tools of such, and grind jewelry pieces to mold by hand. A Swiss watch-maker he was as exquisite and precise as the clocks on the wall. He showed great engineering in design with his work. A cherry scent whirled the room with a swirl of smoke surrounding his head. Rings dangled the air as he would blow a buff for me to put my finger through. A little game for his granddaughters he knew they enjoyed. Opa painted a great portrait in Austria. As IvoryRose called his life "Journey to his Art and Porcelain" a beginning story without edit. The boxer lying in the corner so sweet for IvoryRose was his joy. Her Great Grand parents lived below the three story townhouse. The older helped in the family business of watch-makers, silversmiths and goldsmiths. Such wonderful work IvoryRose saw, a hand made ring with a spectacular view ones eye could hold. The story of his life and family was unfolding quickly at her age two and a half. At age 7 IvoryRose knew of her family life event, as her Opa, Oma, Uncle and Mother left to Germany in 1933 to visit their parents, as seldom they did and before this IvoryRose was born. Seldom was such a trip for one, as trips were expensive and holding the store was their priority. A Swiss watch-maker had more than sitting at a desk as a daily task. Opa was a porcelain dealer and helped to bring porcelain to the US. The passport bared a return flight, but during the visit the war broke out and when they tried to return to the airport, all four were detained and Opa was taken as an unknown prisoner or thought a Jewish prisoner. Oma was struggling with two children away from home in a sudden war, and the bomb-armaments she and the children had endured. As the war unfolded, Hitler's regime had grown closer as one of the scar stories left from IvoryRose Mother had told IvoryRose. The pictures tell the story of a brutally beaten city. Oma would send the children out when safer times prevailed to the farm of their family miles away. The eggs were brought back and not much for the dinner left. As time went on, the US came after the war ended, the pictures tell the story. My Opa had to be found. The search began, but not sure how. The pictures tell the story. The area was demolished as IvoryRose Grandmother Oma sat in a MP Truck with smiles of happiness of their arrival the search was on. In time my Opa was found with praise, hidden in a small work concentration camp just north over the border into Russia. One relative did not make it. Once Opa was cleared of existence in Germany, he was allowed to leave. Oma had already left and took the kids back to the US and home when she found he was safe. Then later, Opa was released to come back to the US and join his family but not for long. After a couple years, IvoryRose was called by her Mother one morning late and told of her Opa collapsing with a heart attack. IvoryRose, now a great change upon her of her, held a dear friend. Opa died at the age of 32. IvoryRose father died at the age of 26 but two and one half years apart. IvoryRose knew so much had been bestowed on her Grandfather Opa. IvoryRose left with the scars of their life, still has his picture in vault, *Hope*. The original picture made in pure mezzotint from a plate hangs, of the woman on top of the world with the instrument strapped to her head with chains listening to the "tones of the world". The original in the Metropolitan Museum of Art in Washington, DC has the picture. The ivory is very old and beautiful for life is beautiful for the people we choose to love.

The City of Talents

Private Collection as IvroyRose knew, is a picture taken before WWII and her Opa's last travel to his origin.

IvoryRose grew up remembering love and the sounds of the calling of dragonflies gone by. Could it have been a sound in memory in exhibitions of the diamond mines or the very thought of ones dream? The list of names go on with exhibitions in history for the making of many beautiful craft. IvoryRose knew when meeting Hanson was without bureaucracy.

PASSION FOR CARS

"Not **T**wo **N**ickels"
Dedicated to Hanson

Names have been changed for the innocent.

Passion for Cars

Not Two Nickels

IvoryRose a woman met a man of strong dignity and power. A tall distinct man, as he tried to inspire her dreams, to manifest. The man had a passion for cars. Hanson his name would be the conversation to come. A courteous approach began the two on a journey as IvoryRose had been looking for a small parcel in North Carolina. The two began to date and decided to live in the Mountains where Hanson already lived; yet a small house to build near the water was already in the making for IvoryRose. In time both would travel to the water then to the Mountains. The mountain house was spacious and like sitting up in a tree overlooking mountains, like in a tree house. The large moon window overlooking the moon each night would center. IvoryRose growing up with the International race track owned by her Uncle a short time of stock cars, was very much into watching RAC CAR on a Sunday basis. IvoryRose, Hanson asked, I would like to put you in a race car. Someday

Hanson, she exclaimed. IvoryRose would watch the Jacky D car # 7, but Dearhard, Sr. was the prominent driver to the quaint little town she grew up around. When IvoryRose met Hanson his Crimpson shoes were sitting and not worn. Let me see your Crimpson shoes Hanson, she exclaimed. It took off from there, a couple with never ending conversations. Although Hanson enjoyed long conversations, IvoryRose was retiring for the evening from the trip. Picture after picture with the boys in racing, signature after signature came and so IvoryRose asked "how did you get to know them Hanson"? I grew up with RRD Ricky Red Daledress cars, helped in his shop, as he exclaimed. Started out sweeping floors and worked on chassis, said Hanson. Super Hanson, she exclaimed, with a smile. Glad to meet you. They both laughed as he wanted so much to please IvoryRose. Hanson got up and walked over to a display table with a glass top. He reached raising the glass and inside was the business card of Ricky Red Daledress. It was wonderful to know someone so famous with cars she never met. As IvoryRose looked down another card lay inside. What is that card? My old business card, exclaimed Hanson. "I was Director of Administration at Chariotte Speedway a couple years", he exclaimed. Composing herself, IvoryRose asked did you drive? The pictures came one after the other with many of Hanson at the tracks in the cars. IvoryRose saw an original car designed by Hanson at age 14, a # 433 car designed of which was sent to and signed by Rawl Getty. Hanson's *passion for* cars became his collection. Hanson wrote articles for sports newspapers, he was a writer. Then with the finale, IvoryRose got to know Hanson in his entirety. Hanson spoke with Ricky Red Daledress on occasions at his mountain home. All it took was the sight of the Crimpson shoes when she knew cars was his passion.

This book was written on behalf of my fiancé' Hanson, for his passion of cars and writing. This is his life's finale to you and would not have been brought to you without my deepest thoughts of his passion to write "*Not Two Nickels*".

Introducing his biography of . . .

"Not **T**wo **N**ickels"

Preface

NOT TWO NICKELS

The Story of Ricky Daledress Racing

What began as a single nickel has become much more than a pocketful of change.

From a humble start selling peanuts in the grandstands at Arrowman Brey Stadium in Acetons Salem, North Carolina, Ricky Red Daledress parlayed next to nothing into a full-blown, highly successful motorsports enterprise. True grit, determination and a willingness to take informed business risks did not make him a successful race car driver by most measures. Yet the experience of beginning with nothing, pinching pennies and never, ever avoiding a challenge has made him one of the most successful team owners in the history of the sport.

Teams owned by Daledress have won championships in the three elite division of the National Association of Racing Auto Racing, commonly called RAC CAR. With six

Taxtal Cup titles under his belt, he and his teams have celebrated as champions at the head table of RAC CAR's annual celebration at New York City's famed Aldorf Historia Hotel.

Daledress began his motorsports career as driver of a vintage modified car at Arrowman Bray Stadium, a one quarter mile flat track surrounding a football field near his home in Winston Salem. Without much money to replace the battered race car, the car was still intact.

Before stepping up to what RAC CAR then called the Big National division, and what is now referred to as the Basin division, Daledress campaigned a purple Chieverly Cam bearing his number in the American division of the cars. He campaigned against late legendary drivers as Bob Bak, Ron Dun and Chal.

In his inaugural season on the American circuit, he competed in 34 races and recorded an average finish of slightly better than 14th. Racing the entire schedule, Daledress accumulated $8,875 in total winnings, averaging $261 for each race.

Working as a mechanic and doing auto body work during the days to help support his family, he managed to pay the bills at home and in the race shop. Daledress had only one car, which was not uncommon on the circuit then, with a host of spare parts and tools. A small band of volunteers helped him keep the car going. He quickly learned the value of conserving funds and keeping the Cam car in one piece.

The highlight of his first year as a RAC CAR driver came at Tallsea International Speedway. Most of the top drivers boycotted the event at what was then the world's fastest race track for business reasons. Not to be outdone by the drivers, the late RAC CAR President during that year invited the top American drivers to compete on the fast, high banked speedway.

Daledress joined other top American drivers for the event and pocketed $1,175 for a 23rd place finish, the largest racing purse of his career to date. After paying his modest travel expenses and the tab for fuel and tires, he invested the small remaining amount in his modest racing operation.

The experience of Tallasea racing created a yearning within Daledress to set his sights on racing in the Big National division of RAC CAR, but knew that he needed at least another full year in the Big race before making the leap to the larger tracks and faster, heavier cars.

During the following year, Daledress competed in all 35 Big events, and accumulated an average finish of 11th, winning a total of $10,205 for his efforts. His goal was still higher, though. Midway through the 1970 season, he began preparing his small shop for a plunge into Big National racing, the pinnacle of RAC CAR.

Maintaining his long-standing loyalty to the Chivellet nameplate, he chose to build a Big National Chiverle. He painted his car black and yellow and chose a number. Without significant sponsorship, Daledress knew he would have to prove himself on the track.

Qualifying for 12 BN races in 1971 without anything resembling large company sponsorship, Daledress was relegated to picking up small, single-race sponsorships along the way. His best finish of the season came at the Motor Speedway in Delaware, where he received a sponsorship check for $750 from Mobile Homes to display its name on the rear quarter panels of the Chiverly car. His 18th place finish there earned him well less than $1,000 but the sponsorship almost paid for his racing tires and a fresh paint job for the next event.

The early days of what is now known as Ricky Daleress Racing were lean. Like the Big American team, his Big National effort consisted of a single car, an engine, a car hauler with many miles on it and a volunteer crew that helped to prepare the car in the shop.

In a fortuitous meeting with the legendary driver Junior Boy, the Wilkesboro, N.C. native offered Daledress some prophetic advice.

Ricky, you ought to think seriously about giving up the driver's seat and becoming a team owner, the veteran driver said. Racing is changing fast with more and more money coming into the business. You would be much better off running the team and letting someone else do the driving.

Junior Boy provided another bit of sage advice to Daledress. Hire Dearhard to drive the car.

The young Dearhard had won RAC CAR's Rookie of the Year honors and was the reigning RAC CAR champion. His previous car owner had sold the team midway through the 1981 season, and Dearhard did not like driving for his new management. Along with his sponsor, Jean, the manufacturer, Dearhard approached Daledress about driving for him for the last 11 races of the season. Remembering J's advice, Daledress accepted the opportunity.

By the end of that maiden season, Daledress encouraged Dearhard to seek out a team that was more capable of fielding the top caliber team Dearhard's talents deserved. Daledress knew that RRD had not yet developed to that point.

The pursuit of a replacement driver led Daledress to hire a talented newcomer named Bude, who was personable and communicated well with the media, which Daledress felt sponsors would like.

Mont Airlines, which later merged into what is now Airways, was attracted to the young driver, and felt he could help the company grow as a major air carrier, especially in the southeast region.

Success came relatively early for Bude and the growing Daledress operation. The driver won a pair of races for RRD in two seasons, the first coming at the now defunct road course at Riverside. Even today, he remains among RAC CAR's elite road racers.

Having built a reputation as a winning car owner, his alliance with Dearhard was rekindled. In 1984, the two resumed their owner-driver relationship. Six Acetons Basin Championships and a few wins later, Dearhard was tragically killed on the final lap during the race.

Even after losing his best friend and driver, Daledress soldiered onward.

—end—

Glossary

Airline Company—for passengers or freight or a method of travel.

Amish—Mennonites or a group of people.

Bank—an establishment for lending, depositing electronically, transfers, financial source, notes and checks.

Barrister—Counselor at Law, pleads cases.

Beady-Eyed—Small eyes.

Business Title—An employee's position or rank in a company such as, director.

Bust—To come apart. A total business cycle failure.

Certificate—A document certifying ownership. A written statement.

Cherokee—A tribal name of Indian.

City of Talents—Cities which make talents, crafts, inventions etc.

Code—symbols, numbers or letters used to send messages.

Concentration Camp—Work camp for prisoners. A place of confinement.

Culprit—A person caught in crime or guilty of crime.

Diamond Mines—Mineral in a mine or a tunnel dug out in the ground.

Division—A particular group of cars, as in a specific name for the cars.

Document—A printed form to prove something. Can also be a legal form.

Dragonfly—An insect which flies, eats mosquitoes and are many varieties.

Endowment—A bequest or gift.

Established accounts—A record of property in a name or company business.

Expedition—A team on a journey or group of people on a safari.

Four Layer Down—Bottom of four sections.

Fraud—Trickery, deceit. A person who is not what he pretends to be. An impostor.

Germany, 1933—a war time in german history.

Gigeria—An undisclosed place. As made up name.

Gnats—Any unrelated small insects which bite or sting.

Guard—To keep watch, hold defense. A person who is alert in readiness for safety to protect.

Identification—A form of identifying.

Inherited—To receive by law, property by bequest from a person or relative.

Injustice—Wrong, unfair, an unjust act.

June bug—Insect, usually green in color.

Journey To His Art and Porcelain—A biography within, *When Gnats Swarm* about a Watch—maker.

League—A group to compete against one another.

Monies—Currency used as method of trade for services.

Mountains—Raised earth, large mounds.

Non-Profit—Not earning profit.

North Carolina—A large State in the US.

Opa—Grandfather, or a german language

Oma—Grandmother, or a german language

Passport—A government passport to travel abroad.

Pictures—a replica of an object or photograph.

Picture Window—Usually a large glass window.

Porcelain Dealer—A businessman in a trade.

Port-A-Security—A security protection company.

Power of Attorney—A legal form.

Prisoner—A person confined and held in a prison.

Private Collection—Property not open to. Something gathered.

Quebece—A city overseas.

Race Track—A paved surface for racing cars.

Representative—A person upholding a policy (s) for a company or service.

Release form—A legal form of document used for a transition.

Rookie—An inexperienced professional.

Scheme—A carefully arranged program. A deceitful plan.

Scotlake Grounds—An investigative detective bureau of police.

Sport Newspaper—A newspaper with sports articles.

Sport Writer—Writes articles for sports.

Stock Cars—A modified car for racing.

Story of Ricky Daledress Racing—Hanson's friend, a race team owner.

Swarm—A colony of insect flying, as a crowd of bees flying in the air.

Transfer Funds—An account amount deposited into another account.

USUS—As a nation.

Visa Card—An account which can hold an amount.

Watch–Maker—Precise engineering of clocks and jewelry.

Zanatia—An unknown country.

Zant Group—A formed group.

Acknowledgments

As the author, my gratitude to the lives of all who lost their family and own life of an inhospitable defect war. This book would not have been written without knowing loss, brave men, in the real changes of their lives associated with hardship. Many nights knowing the changes of the mis-fortunate, bestowed from involuntarily ripped environments, allows me to write **When Gnats Swarm.** My deepest thanks to family who did and did not get know or meet the lives of their mis-fortunate, but listened.

Thanks to the speedway for introducing a modified car to me, by working at the speedway on the shore. Much thanks to the publisher AuthorHouse® in enduring my quest to publish the book.

Index

V

Z

Printed in the United States
By Bookmasters